D1562075

CINDY STEINBECK

GRAPES
of
Grace

**I am the vine; you are
the branches.** John 15:5

CONCORDIA PUBLISHING HOUSE • SAINT LOUIS

To you, fellow lovers of the vineyard and The Vine.

CS

Published 2015 by Concordia Publishing House
3558 S. Jefferson Avenue, St. Louis, MO 63118-3968
1-800-325-3040 · www.cph.org

Manufactured in Heshan,China

1 2 3 4 5 6 7 8 9 10   24 23 22 21 20 19 18 17 16 15

6 abide   34 grow   70 work   100 heal   128 rest

Jesus provides rich imagery and meaning when He says, "Abide in Me, and I in you" and "I am the vine; you are the branches" (John 15:4, 5).

Jesus spoke the words to His disciples in the Upper Room in the confusing, challenging days just prior to His arrest and crucifixion. His passion for keeping His own close to Him in the midst of trying times is evident in the vine imagery. John recorded these words for us, for today. These words call us to grow in faith in the One who calls us to abide in His life.

Abide means to dwell, to remain, to stay, to have one's abode, or to continue in a particular attitude or relationship. Abiding "in Christ" means that He is our dwelling place. We are grafted into His holy life when we come to faith in Him; we live in Christ now, and we live in Christ for eternity. Therefore, His life is our abiding place, and we live in relationship with Him.

These words from John 15 are alive for me because I live and work among the vines in my vineyard. The photos in this book, taken in my vineyard during different seasons and stages of growth, will show you the beauty I see. In these photos and through the words on these pages, you will grow—as I have—in understanding of His work for us and in us and through us.

The Vine—Jesus—speaks these profound images through the roots, the sap flow, the canes, the buds, the leaves, and the fruit. Meaningful imagery unfolds when we see the work of the vine on the branches and in the fruit. The narrative of the vine also shows, in rich Old Testament imagery, the relationship between God the Father (the Vinedresser) and the Son (the Vine).

The branches receive the work of the vinedresser in order to be healthy and grow and bear much fruit. A grapevine's bearing fruit is the natural result of healthy branches on a healthy vine, and a Christian's bearing fruit is the natural result of abiding in Christ's holy life. His life keeps us, cleanses us, provides nutrients and water; His life gives life and promotes growth. Health means embracing ourselves and those around us as multifaceted, wonderfully created human beings, whose lives are precious to God, the one who breathed His life into our being. He calls us to live, to life; He calls us to grow.

Growing means change, and change can be challenging. Sometimes we endure a pruning when God calls us to recognize our sin and to change. We fight it, but in faith we cling to the promise of the Vine's life in us and our life in Him. We are grafted into Christ's life; we are rooted and grounded in Him. We are alive in the Vine, and He is alive in us.

My prayer is that the images and the words on these pages be for your encouragement and hope in the True Vine, as they have been for me. I invite you to step into my vineyard and journey with me into deeper faith and trust in Him through the vines.

Cindy Steinbeck

$\mathcal{A}$bide in Me, and I in you.

As the branch cannot bear fruit by itself,

unless it abides in the vine, neither can you,

unless you abide in Me.

I am the vine; you are the branches.

Whoever abides in Me and I in him,

he it is that bears much fruit,

for apart from Me you can do nothing.

John 15:4–5

This 33-year-old vine has
grown to form the shape c
the crucifix: arms lifted up
the face of Christ hanging
down and to the right, the
body and legs in the trunk

Are we human beings
or human doings?

Does our being define our doing,
or does our doing define our being?

Our value in this life comes from being. We are human beings, valued because we are alive. Because we are redeemed by the precious blood of Christ and cherished by Him, we can do the work He calls us to do.

300,000 grapevines adorn the hills of Steinbeck Vineyards in Paso Robles, California.

Paul says that the energy of God at work in us is the same energy that raised Jesus from the dead! The sap flow in every plant is moving, bringing

water and nutrients—energy—to the vines.
Christ's life in us breeds life, breeds energy for us.
We work and we rest in that life.

He Himself bore our sins in His body on the tree,
that we might die to sin and live to righteousness.
By His wounds you have been healed.

1 Peter 2:24

A knife, a bandage, and a single little bud are the necessary elements of grafting on to root-stock. The rootstock is not susceptible to disease and provides a home for the varietals we choose for our vine-yard. Christ is the stock into whose holy life we, the branches, are graft-ed. His life is our home, our abiding place. No matter where we live, we live "in Christ."

$\mathcal{W}$hoever confesses that
Jesus is the Son of God,
God abides in Him,
and he in God.

1 John 4:15

Oma's tree was planted
in memory of Grandma
Steinbeck in 2007.

And what is the immeasurable greatness
of His power toward us who believe,
according to the working of His great might
that He worked in Christ when He raised
Him from the dead and seated Him at His
right hand in the heavenly places.

Ephesians 1:19–20

Teach us, O God, to be receivers, to hear and to learn according to Your desires for us. Direct us, guide us in Your Word, and hold us as we grow up in You. In Jesus' precious name. Amen.

Vineyard owner Ryan Newkirk discusses best practices in the vineyard with eager listeners.

Focus means to fix our eyes or attention on a single point. Focusing on God's work for us and in us deserves not only our full attention but also our faith and trust. He is for us and in us, and His life flows through us.

New spring growth on vines that have rested during the winter months.

lift up my eyes to the hills. From where does my help come? My help comes from the LORD, who made heaven and earth. He will not let your foot be moved; He who keeps you will not slumber. Behold, He who keeps Israel will neither slumber nor sleep. The LORD is your keeper; the LORD is your shade on your right hand. The sun shall not strike you by day, nor the moon by night. The LORD will keep you from all evil; He will keep your life. The LORD will keep your going out and your coming in from this time forth and forevermore.

Psalm 121

Abiding fruit
is Christ's call.
Fruit that abides
is the natural result
of our abiding
relationship in
Christ, as branches
of a fruitful vine.

Cabernet Sauvignon
vines bear fruit,
ripe for the harvest.

abide **27**

Maturity in life is defined by many factors. God's Word calls us to be mature in Christ, to be mature in heart, soul, and spirit. The maturing process continues throughout life in Christ, the True Vine.

Ripe Viognier.

We live today's precious moments,
drawing wisdom and perspective
from life's valuable lessons, with
eyes constantly fixed on eternity
in Christ.

Eternity in Christ is now and forever.

Now may our Lord Jesus Christ Himself, and God our Father, who loved us and gave us eternal comfort and good hope through grace, comfort your hearts and establish them in every good work and word.

2 Thessalonians 2:16–17

God's call on our lives is that we grow
and be restored in all seasons of life.

He brings growth; He restores, flowing from
the intimate relationship of vine to branch.

Our parents taught us;
their parents taught them.
We embrace the healthy.
We identify the unhealthy and let it go.
That is the process of growing.

Growing in faith, understanding,
and love is God's design for life in Him.

The world says, "Conform."

The Word says, "Be transformed."

Transformation and renewal is God's work,
God's action for us and in us.

The work of God, the Master Gardener, the Vinedresser of our lives, is a process He directs. Trust says, "God, You direct the work and cause the growth in Your way and in Your time. I will heed Your call."

The months-long process of preparing the soil and the field are complete; the day for planting the young vines has come.

God is at work at all times
for us and in us. Our hearts and
lives testify to His mighty work—
preparing, planting, causing
growth, training, and even
pruning. It is God who multiplies
faith and hope and love.

A tractor "rips" the soil five feet deep in preparation for planting young vines. This necessary step allows the roots of the vines to penetrate deep into the soil.

*S*earch me, O God, and know my heart!

Try me and know my thoughts!

And see if there be any grievous way in me,

and lead me in the way everlasting!

Psalm 139:23–24

Our souls thirst for living water;
our spirits hunger for growth;
our hearts crave life and aliveness.

Water and Word, bread and wine
are the means by which Christ
connects us to Himself, by which
He sustains us in faith.

My mouth shall speak wisdom;
the meditation of my heart shall be understanding.

Psalm 49:3

...nlight glistens
... the flowing
...p that keeps
... pruning
...und clean until
... cab forms.
...e energy of
...e vine brings
...trients to
...e new buds
...early spring.

grow

According to the riches of His glory He may grant you to be strengthened with power through His Spirit in your inner being, so that Christ may dwell in your hearts through faith—that you, being rooted and grounded in love, may have strength to comprehend with all the saints what is the breadth and length and height and depth, and to know the love of Christ that surpasses knowledge, that you may be filled with all the fullness of God.

Ephesians 3:16–19

Profound conversations of the heart
are the desire of a people created
by a conversational God.
God speaks through His Word;
we speak our hearts in prayer to God;
we speak to one another in Christ's love.

Jesus, You say that in this world
we will have trouble, but to take heart
because You have overcome the world.
At times, it feels like the world is overtaking us!
In those times, give us courage to cling
to You with arms that reach out to no other
and with eyes fixed firmly on You and
the work You have done for us and in us.

Amen.

Each stage of life is "fruit bearing," and some periods of growth are more delicate than others. Look carefully at the "fruit" on this old vine. Tiny flowers containing pollens have burst open during this delicate season called "bloom." High winds, rain, or extreme weather can have a negative effect on this important season.

$\mathcal{I}$n Him we live
and move and
have our being.

Acts 17:28

Grapes turn from green to purple as the energy of the vine shifts from cane and leaf production to sugar production.

Each breath we breathe is an
opportunity to give thanks for
our breath and for the Breath
of Life, who breathes life in us.
Each sip of water we take
gives us opportunity to give
thanks for the One who satisfies
our thirst with His Living Water.
Each bite of bread we take
gives us opportunity to give
thanks for the Bread of Life,
who feeds us with His life
through the Lord's Supper.

Worrying narrows possibilities to what we know and what we can see. Seeking God in His Word, through His people, and in the Vine opens rich possibilities.

Ripening Cabernet Sauvignon hanging until maturity.

The fruit of the Spirit is love, joy, peace, patience, kindness, goodness, faithfulness, gentleness, self-control; against such things there is no law.

Galatians 5:22–23

Picking ripe Cabernet in September.

God, You hold our past,
present, and future in
Your hands, in Your
Son's holy life.
May we be captured
by Your mercy, not
captivated by fear
or worry or guilt
or shame. Renew and
free us; breed life in us.
In Jesus' name. Amen.

Finding our voice comes through listening to the Word of God, heeding God's call to grow up in Him, and embracing the journey in this life. Answering hard questions, leaning into fears, and journeying with others leads to growth.

Gracious heavenly Father, Creator
of heaven and earth, Creator of the vine, speak
Your Word of truth into our hearts and lives.

Even as You show us Your Law and bring us to repentance, You bring growth and understanding of Your love and mercy toward us. Give us courage to receive and, in receiving, the courage to give. In Jesus' precious name. Amen.

$\mathcal{Y}$ou did not choose Me,
but I chose you and appointed
you that you should go and
bear fruit and that your fruit
should abide, so that whatever
you ask the Father in My name,
He may give it to you.

John 15:16

Ripe Cabernet
Sauvignon
ready to be
picked into bins.

Mature hearts and lives
produce mature fruit—
lasting fruit.

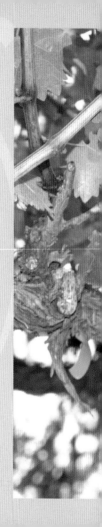

Teach us, O God,
to walk in Your ways,
to listen to Your call
to love deeply, to ask
in expectant hope, and
to bear fruit in keeping
with Your will. In Jesus'
precious name. Amen.

Cabernet Sauvignon
grapes hanging to
maturity before harvest.

Balance in the vineyard,
as in life, brings forth
quality fruit.

Picking Viognier, September.

I am the true vine, and My Father is the vinedresser. Every branch in Me that does not bear fruit He takes away, and every branch that does bear fruit He prunes, that it may bear more fruit.

John 15:1–2

Howie Steinbec
pruning Cabern
vines in January

God is at work in us;
God is at work through us.

Jesus' disciples craved a neat and tidy life as they journeyed with Him thousands of years ago. Instead, their path with Him was sticky, messy, untidy. What do we crave?

Ripe Petite Sirah.

work **83**

In Mark 10, Jesus asks,
"What do you want
Me to do for you?"

Mark 10:36

Will we answer like James and
John or like blind Bartimaeus?

$\mathcal{W}$hatever you ask the Father in My name,

He may give it to you . . .

John 15:16

work **87**

Christ, the Vine, brings growth
and fruitfulness to His vineyard,
the Church, through His Word and work.

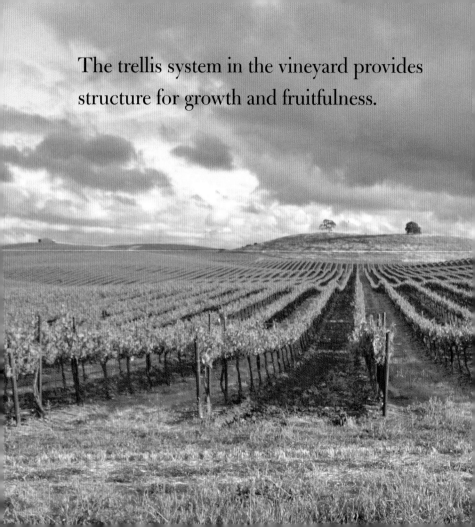

The trellis system in the vineyard provides structure for growth and fruitfulness.

The Law of God opens our eyes to the need for the gifts of the True Vine—forgiveness, mercy, life.

STEINBECK
VINEYARD
PASO
ROBLES CA

God is designer, artist, and builder.
His works are amazing!

*T*he works of God and teachings of God
are established forever and ever with a
purpose: "to be performed with faithfulness
and uprightness" by His people.

Psalm 111:7–8

$\mathcal{F}$or we are His workmanship,
created in Christ Jesus for good works,
which God prepared beforehand,
that we should walk in them.

Ephesians 2:10

Picking Petite Sirah

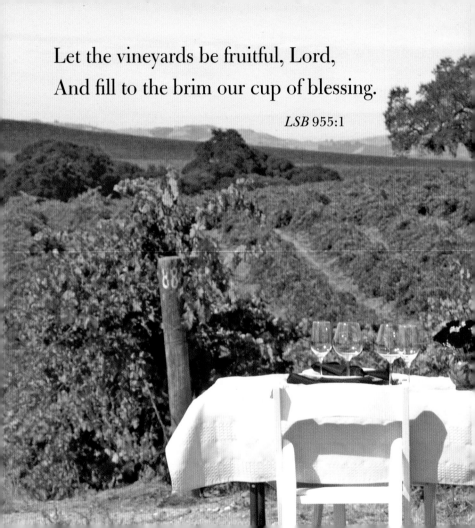

Let the vineyards be fruitful, Lord,
And fill to the brim our cup of blessing.

LSB 955:1

Gracious heavenly Father, the skies declare Your glory! May we with humble hearts come to repentance, receive Your gifts, and reflect Your light in this world, so people might see our good works and glorify You. In Jesus' precious name. Amen!

You brought a vine out of Egypt;
You drove out the nations and planted it.
You cleared the ground for it;
it took deep root and filled the land.
Turn again, O God of hosts!
Look down from heaven, and see;
have regard for this vine,
the stock that Your right hand planted,
and for the Son whom You
made strong for Yourself.

Psalm 80:8–9, 14–15

We are, by God's call and by God's grace, His; salvation is ours. We know where we are going. We know how we're getting there: in and through Christ's mercy, forgiveness, and love. With these truths in mind and heart, we journey more fully into everyday life. Really? Truly? Fully? May God grant us courage to live truly and fully.

COURAGE:

the strength of the mind,
heart, and spirit to face challenges;
to look fear in the eye and overcome.

*B*e strong and courageous. Do not fear
or be in dread of them, for it is the LORD
your God who goes with you.
He will not leave you or forsake you.

Deuteronomy 31:6

Courage and humility are necessary as we take life step by step. We've never taken these same steps before; each one is new. Life is an adventure. Our soul confesses that we don't know what we don't know, and with eyes and heart wide open, with courage and humility, we allow God to guide our steps and make the path straight.

Our eyes and hearts see God's
handiwork for us and in us.
Our lives reflect the richness
of God's mercy in everything
we say and do.

Our hearts jump at the possibility of God restoring our soul, but is it possible? Yes. By faith, we believe that even as we recognize the hopelessness of our sin, a full and complete restoration is reality. Scripture calls us to cling to the truth: we are restored in Jesus today and to eternity.

Faith to move mountains is a gift that originates in and flows from being deeply rooted and grounded in Christ's life. What mountains need to be moved? Fear, unhealthy self-talk, unhealthy relationships, bad habits?

This giant oak's root growth down toward nutrients and water mirrors its growth upward toward the sunlight.

The mountain that is our heart needs to be moved to respond to God's mercy and love in Christ Jesus. By faith, we are called to confess that all things are possible—called to declare God's Word and work is for us, in us, and through us.

$\mathscr{F}$or You formed my inward parts;
You knitted me together in my mother's
womb. I praise You, for I am fearfully
and wonderfully made. Wonderful are
Your works; my soul knows it very well.

Psalm 139:13–14

There is a special place in my vineyard where I and others pause and pray. Then we leave a stone representing a burden we're choosing to give to God. The pause is a deliberate focus. The prayer is a humble, pleading cry to learn how to give that burden to God and to leave it there rather than try to carry it.

Row 124 is a place for transparency and tears, conversation and hugs; a place for quiet, personal reflection.

Christ grafted us into His life in Holy Baptism. He nourishes us in His Holy Supper.

Christ's lifeblood flowed for us and flows in us, continually bringing restoration and healing. Healing in Christ is real, true, and complete.

Sap flows from a pruned vine until a scab forms over the wound.

Perfect vision sees Christ for who He is, what He has done, and what He is doing right here, right now. Jesus attended to the whole person when He walked this earth. His Word and work restored mind, body, soul, heart, and spirit. Jesus attends to our whole person today.

Embrace the journey into Christ's restoration! The disconnect between knowledge of the truth and fully living the truth can be vast and painful. The reality of our brokenness, and the brokenness of the people in this world, is that living fully gets stuck somewhere between our heart's desire and our lack of skill to interpret our emotions, which are often buried, and the accompanying behaviors. Embrace Christ; embrace restoration!

Therefore, as you received Christ Jesus the Lord, so walk in Him, rooted and built up in Him

and established in the faith, just as you were taught,
abounding in thanksgiving.

Colossians 2:6–7

Beyond imagination, O God, are Your works
for us and in us. May we, in all circumstances
and with humble hearts, give thanks that
You have called us to life in Your holy life.
In Jesus' precious name. Amen.

He who dwells in the shelter of the Most High will abide in the shadow of the Almighty. I will say to the LORD, "My refuge and my fortress, my God, in whom I trust."

Psalm 91:1–2

Row 124 in my vineyard has become a place to unburden and be reminded that God wants us to trust Him. Visitors write on a stone and give that burden to God in prayer, resting in the Lord's promises.

*S*o then, there remains
a Sabbath rest for
the people of God,
for whoever has
entered God's rest
has also rested from his works
as God did from His.

Hebrews 4:9–10

Dormant vines resting during winter.

Resting is not "doing nothing."
Resting fulfills God's creative
design as well as teaches us
about our need to rest in Him
who is our rest.

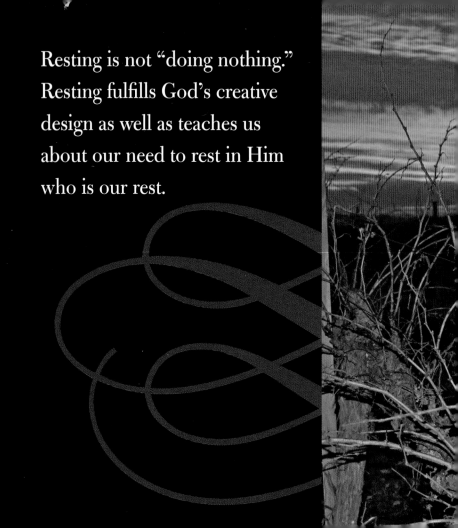

rest

Our deep longing for
rest is created by God.
That longing is filled
when we rest and work in
His gift of life in Christ.
Christ is our rest.
As we rest and as we work,
we do so in His holy life.

In Christ is life and light. He created us as complex individuals with basic needs— and with an inborn need for Him. We rest when we rest in Him; we breathe when we breathe in Him; we work when we work in Him. He is the "more" we are looking for. Christ is life and light.

This giant oak overlooks Steinbeck Vineyards. Find the heart in the tree branches, middle left.

Gracious heavenly Father, teach us during sleepless nights to rest well in Your mercy

and to cast our cares on You, who cares
deeply for us. In Jesus' precious name. Amen.

Light wins.

The light shines, and darkness fades away.

Sunrise and sunset,
the beginning and
ending of each day,
offer us opportunity
to pause,
to praise,
to pray.

...easured the waters in the hollow

...and marked off the heavens with a s...

...ust of the earth in a measure

...weighed the mountains in scales

and the hills in a balance?

Who has measured the Spirit of the LORD,

or what man shows Him His counsel?

Isaiah 40:12–13

In this is love, not that we have loved God
but that He loved us and sent His Son
to be the propitiation for our sins.
Beloved, if God so loved us, we also ought
to love one another. No one has ever seen
God; if we love one another, God abides
in us and His love is perfected in us.

1 John 4:10–12

God's promises,
complete in Christ,
are for us.

God, grant us courage
to cling to You and
to Your promises.
In Jesus' precious name.
Amen.